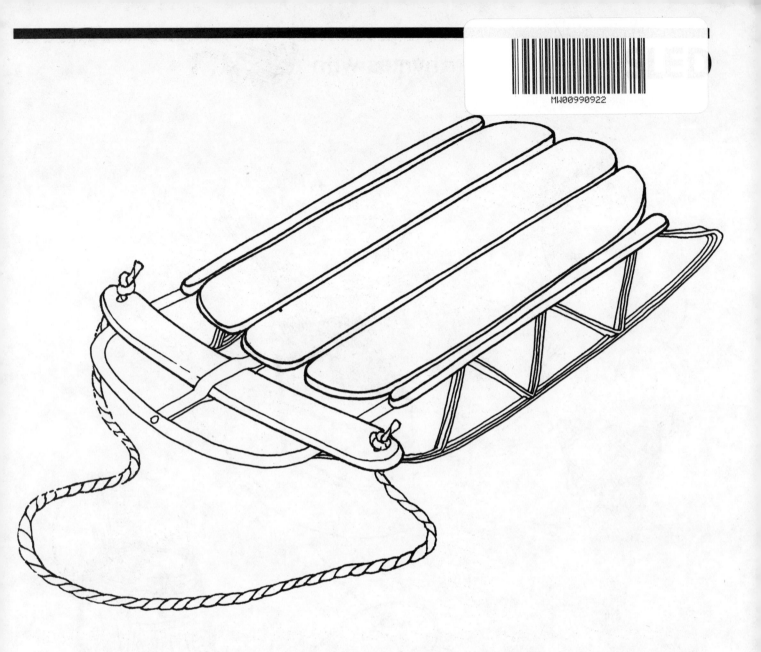

Circle the picture that rhymes with the big one.

Circle the picture that rhymes with .

Circle the picture that rhymes with the big one.

Circle the picture that rhymes with .

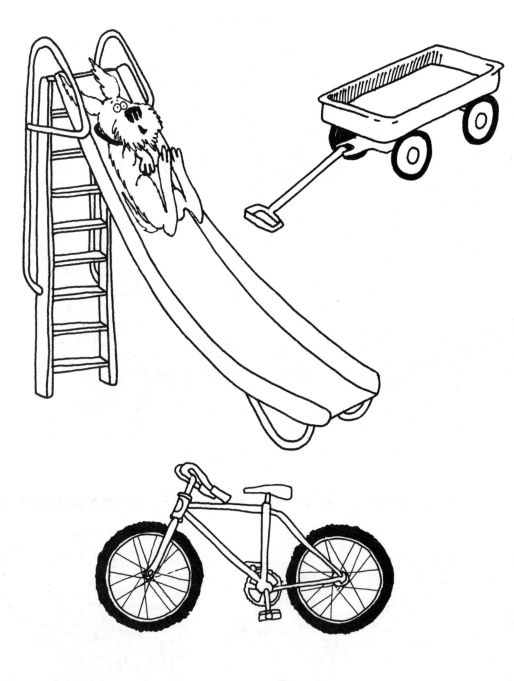

BELL

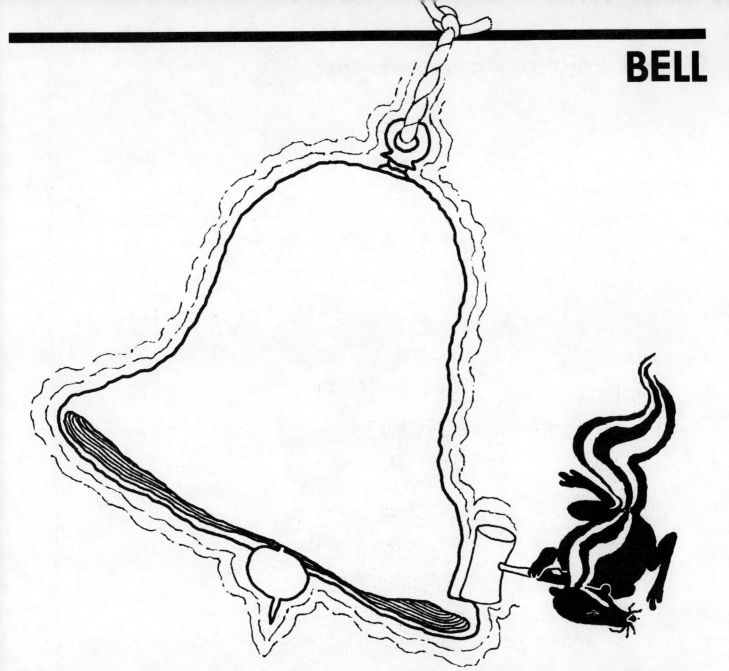

Circle the picture that rhymes with the big one.

Circle the picture that rhymes with .

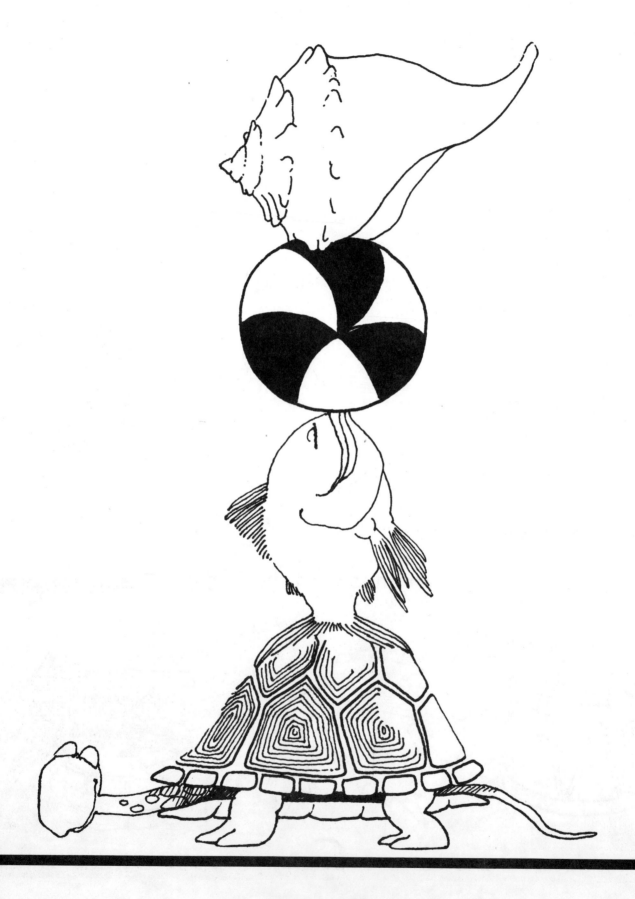

Circle the picture that rhymes with the big one.

Circle the picture that rhymes with  .

CLOCK

Circle the picture that rhymes with the big one.

11

Circle the picture that rhymes with .

BEAR

Circle the picture that rhymes with the big one.

Circle the picture that rhymes with .

Circle the picture that rhymes with the big one. ▬▬▬

Circle the picture that rhymes with .

Circle the picture that rhymes with the big one.

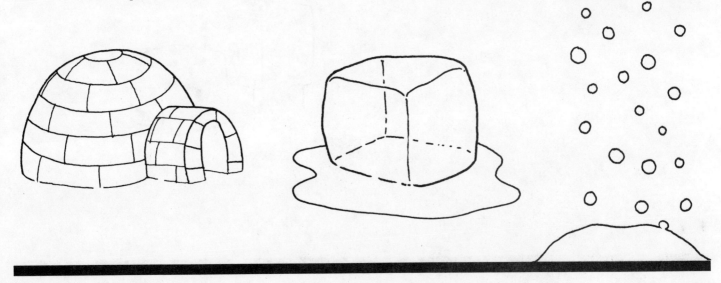

Circle the picture that rhymes with

Circle the picture that rhymes with the big one.

Circle the picture that rhymes with  .

Circle the picture that rhymes with the big one.

Circle the picture that rhymes with .

Circle the picture that rhymes with the big one.

Circle the picture that rhymes with .

COOK

Circle the picture that rhymes with the big one.

DRUM

Circle the picture that rhymes with the big one.

Circle the picture that rhymes with .

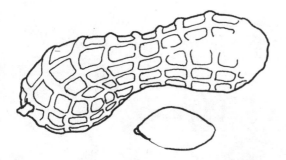

Circle the picture that rhymes with the big one.

Circle the picture that rhymes with .